S0-CFL-718

I FIND REST IN GOD;
ONLY HE GIVES ME HOPE.
**HE IS MY ROCK AND
MY SALVATION. HE
IS MY DEFENDER;**
I WILL NOT
BE DEFEATED.

—PSALM 62:5-6

PRESENTED TO

BY

DATE

Dedicated to my three amazing children:
Hannah, Charity, and Cameron.

**God created you for something great
. . .embrace it and you will discover all that
one person can do to impact the world!**

RON LUCE

THE POWER OF ONE

stand up :: be counted ::
make a difference

CROSSCULTURE™

COUNTRYMAN®
Nashville, Tennessee

Published by J. Countryman, a division of Thomas Nelson, Inc. Nashville, Tennessee 37214

J. Countryman is a trademark of Thomas Nelson, Inc.

All Scripture quotations in this book, unless otherwise indicated, are from the New Century Version (NCV) ©1987, 1988, 1991 by W Publishing Group, Nashville, Tennessee 37214, and are used by permission.

The New King James Version (NKJV) © 1979, 1980, 1982, 1992, Thomas Nelson, Inc., Publisher. Used by permission.

The New International Version of the Bible (NIV) © 1984 by the International Bible Society. Used by permission of Zondervan Bible Publishers.

The Holy Bible, New Living Translation (NLT) © 1996. Used by permission of Tyndale House Publishers, Inc., Wheaton, Ill. All rights reserved.

The King James Version of the Bible (KJV).

Project editor: Kathy Baker

www.thomasnelson.com
www.jcountryman.com

www.teenmania.com
www.acquirethefire.com

Designed by Lookout Design Group, Minneapolis, Minnesota

ISBN: 1-4041-0081-4 softcover
ISBN: 1-4041-0082-2 hardcover

Printed and bound in the United States of America

Contents

Introduction

Introduction

REAL STORIES. REAL POWER.

What you are about to read are real stories from real people who have faced many of the same challenges you have faced—or will face—for taking a stand for your faith. As you read about the unique encounters that these young people have had, imagine yourself in the same positions. Think of the courage your peers had to face the situations and then embrace that courage as your own.

As Christians, Jesus told us this new life was going to take courage. He never promised a walk through the rose gardens in our Christianity. He said it over and over again in a number of different ways: "The gate is wide

and the road is wide that leads to hell, and
many people enter through that gate. But the
gate is small and the road is narrow that leads
to true life. Only a few people find that road"
(Matthew 7:13–14). The reason the path to
destruction is wider is because a lot more
people are on it, and all the people on the wide
path are going to mock those of us on the
narrow path.

As you read the true stories in this book,
you are going to be inspired by young people on
the narrow road. You are going to be encouraged
by those who, in the face of their friends or
family, stood strong even at a young age. I'll
begin most sections by telling you stories from
my own life and the opportunities I had to
stand. Let us take hope in the fact that, as
Hebrews 12:1 says, "that a great cloud of
witnesses" is watching how we respond to the
persecution we endure. That means people like

Peter, James, John, Moses, Elijah, and
Abraham are all watching us, not to mention all
the angels who are cheering us on from heaven.

I pray that as a result of reading these
stories your backbone will be stronger, your
head will be higher, your shoulders will be
straighter, and you'll be able to endure
whatever comes your way in the name of Christ.
I pray that at the end of your life you might
write your own book filled with the same kind
of stories about how you stood up when the
world assaulted your faith.

CONSUMED BY THE CALL,

RON LUCE

My Daily Mission Field:

STANDING UP TO PEER PRESSURE AT SCHOOL

I knew when I got up that fall morning of my twelfth grade year I was going to have to make a decision. Was I going to leave it there on my dresser all day or would I actually put it around my neck and be identified as a follower? It had lain on my dresser for the first two weeks of school, and now the cross that I had worn so proudly all summer while working construction just sat there glaring at me—as if questioning my commitment to the One who had died on it.

This was no ordinary cross. It was a three-inch by four-inch solid iron cross hanging on a rugged chain. I had worn it all that summer; I might not have always worn my shirt while working construction, but I always wore that cross. It didn't matter to me if those construction workers criticized me or called me names. In fact, I wore it proudly to the point where it actually scarred my chest by hitting me repeatedly. But after a summer of such incredible boldness, my cross now sat silently on my dresser.

Thinking that the peer pressure and mockery at school would be too unbearable, too formidable to endure, I had abandoned it. I comforted my conscience by offering excuses like, "I want them to see Jesus in my lifestyle, and then ask me questions."

My pastor took me to school every day because I lived with him most of my senior year (we'll get to that story later in the book). He "happened" to notice that I wasn't wearing my cross. I tried to help him understand that I wanted to "break in my friends slowly" to the fact that I was now a Christian.

He kindly, but confidently, asked, "How do you break them in slowly? You either are a Christian or you're not." The words cut my heart like a knife. Was I now embarrassed to be connected to the very One who changed my life? The words haunted me all that day. I wondered if I would have the courage to wear this outward sign of my faith at school. The admiration of friends seemed more powerful than the admiration of God. Even as I got ready for school that morning, I still had not decided what I was going to do with the cross.

I remember looking in the mirror, looking down again at the cross, looking up again in the mirror, and being pulled once more down to that rugged cross. I wondered, "Is this the beginning of a lifestyle of ashamedly hiding the fact that something dramatic has happened in my heart?"

Little did I know this would be a moment that would define the rest of my life and the kind of Christianity that I would live forever. The look in my eyes as I glared back at myself in the mirror was the look of a weasel; the look of a person who would gladly take, but never give back; the look of a person who would gladly receive forgiveness, but who wasn't sure if he could tell others about the forgiveness that he received. There was a wrestling going on in my own heart. Just how would I carry myself as a Christian?

I knew that I did not have to wear a cross to be a Christian, but wearing it had become normal to me, what I gladly did outside of school. I had no problem wearing this cross on the job, so what was the big deal about wearing it at school? Why was I having such a hard time? As the battle raged in my heart, I could not help but think about the price that was paid by the One who died on that cross. How could I just leave it there?

I decided that I did not want see a weasel in the mirror for the rest of my life. No matter what happened as a result of wearing the cross—no matter how much mockery I might endure—it could not compare to the pain I would feel knowing that I had betrayed the One who gave everything for me.

I reached down, grabbed the chain, and slung it around my neck. For a moment I felt bold. I put my T–shirt on top, and I was ready to walk out the door. But when I glanced back I saw the weasel once again in my eyes. "At least I have it on" wasn't good enough, so watching myself closely, I reached inside of my shirt, pulled out the cross and placed it boldly across my shirt like a Superman insignia.

I did not know what was about to confront me, but I knew that at least I could march to school with a clear conscience, knowing that God was on my side and that I was not ashamed of the One who had set me free. I remember how it felt to walk down the hallway that day at school—I felt like everyone was staring at my chest, like it shined in the darkness amid hundreds of my peers.

This was my defining moment as a young Christian. You are about to read a book full of stories of young men and women who have made this kind of a decision. Some of them are recent stories and some are from the past. You will read about modern-day teen heroes as well as stories of Biblical heroes.

These kinds of decisions define who we are and set the pace for the kinds of Christians that we are going to be for the rest of our lives. People who refuse to give in, who are willing to stand up for their faith in the early years of their lives, find themselves standing strong for many years to come, even into old age.

My prayer is that as you read these stories they would inspire your faith and encourage you to make the right decision when you face your defining moment. Such decisions have transformed thousands of other young people into world-changers for the rest of their lives.

—RON LUCE

Yes, I am sure that neither death, nor life, nor angels, nor ruling spirits, nothing now, nothing in the future, no powers, nothing above us, nothing below us, nor anything else in the whole world will ever be able to separate us from the love of God that is in Christ Jesus our Lord.

—ROMANS 8:38

18

These words are written by a man who was stoned, whipped, thrown into jail and called every name in the book multiple times. In the midst of all of this he was convinced that he was surrounded by God's love always. Take this confidence with you into your school, classroom, and hallway today. It may be against the law to pray or preach in school; they might not allow all kinds of things, but they cannot stop the love of God from surrounding you all day long.

When I was in seventh grade, I realized that I needed to do something drastic to try to reach the older students, many of whom sometimes would push me into my locker or yell at me for my outspoken views of Jesus. I would never force my classmates or other students to listen to my thoughts on Him, but they did and then responded anyway. After a weekend of thinking about this challenge I decided to slip a gospel tract into every student's locker in the high school on Monday before school started. I thought this would be an unobtrusive way to reach the other students or at least get them to think. I honestly doubted anyone would even care; if someone did not want a tract they could just throw it away.

Wow, was I naive in my thinking. You would have thought I sent out pamphlets on how to smoke crack, the way the students responded and then their parents. Fortunately for myself I did not have a reputation as a trouble-maker, so teachers came to my aid. I was instructed that I would have to come before the school board and defend my actions. As it turned out, handing out tracts was against the school rules. Who knew?

I thought the students would be supportive, but in reality the students who in the past had been nice to me suddenly became mean. Some called me names, but then other students asked me questions and some even gave their lives to Jesus. I was never scared or fearful because I knew that God was pleased with me.

I realized afterwards that because I was under authority I should have checked the rules more thoroughly before doing what I did. However, since it was too late to change what I had done, I could see how God used this situation to teach me how to look to Jesus, not others, for love and acceptance. This entire episode definitely drove me closer to Jesus and drove a stake in the ground with my friends.

I learned that you never know who the true lovers of Jesus are until persecution comes. Many of my friends who were not really bad were knocked off the fence that year; some started smoking pot, sleeping with their girlfriends, and so forth. Others decided to pursue Jesus and to this day are living for Him. I look back at that decision to hand out

tracts, and I know it helped everyone realize I
was going to be an obvious Christian.

—DAVID

Everyone who has ever changed the
world has had to step out and do
something unusual.

PEOPLE ARE MAKING
FUN OF ME. LET THEM BE
SHAMED INTO SILENCE.
BUT LET THOSE WHO
FOLLOW YOU BE
HAPPY AND GLAD.
THEY LOVE YOU FOR
SAVING THEM. MAY
THEY ALWAYS SAY,
"PRAISE THE LORD!"

—PSALM 40:15-16

When I was a freshman I decided to take on my school for Christ. There wasn't any support for my cause, so I basically stood alone. Besides the rude gestures and comments made towards me as a Christian, a different type of persecution ensued. I got my Bible study flyers torn down and my locker ransacked. Yet what stood out most was when I decided to pray at the flagpole on the National Day of Prayer. I was on my knees alone at the flagpole when people started to harass me. They swore at me, threatened me, and threw stuff at me. It got to the point where the principal had to stop them. Yet God saw my struggle and that year six of my friends came to know Christ!

Going through that changed me, because it helped me see what was important in an important situation. Doing what's right is unpopular a lot of the time and you might have your reputation ruined. But who am I next to Jesus? He never cared about His reputation; as long as we were paid for, He didn't care about the sacrifice. It also made me realize that other Jesus Freaks have given their lives to do the right thing, so it's no big deal if I get mocked for Jesus. When I stand up for Christ someone might see my devotion and think that maybe it's something worth living for. Going through this experience taught me really what it meant to have conviction. You can believe in something but never really have that belief made real in your heart unless you go through something like this. When you endure persecution, you realize what your faith means to you.

Sometimes I ask myself "Why do you do it?" Then I think about all the people who have given their lives for the Gospel. They had so much faith because they knew that Jesus was behind them. They set the example and let Christ be seen through them. I want my life to be viewed as letting Christ be seen, because when I least expect it or when I want to give up, someone may be changed for the Gospel.

—ELIZABETH

Your endurance could be the vital link to other's salvation!

While we were sitting around during gym one day, some kids started calling me "God boy." The usual guys were already making fun of me, and they were just digging for something new. They found out that I went to church with my parents every week, and thought that would be a good topic to have fun with.

Now, being called names wasn't a new thing for me. But, this name was different. I didn't know a lot about being a Christian then. I didn't even have a close church or friends who were truly living for God. But this persecution inspired me—being made fun of as "God boy" was something I didn't want to disprove, but aspire to.

I asked God to show me more of Himself. At the time, I didn't know any Scriptures, but it pushed me to begin reading. It eventually inspired me to live a Christ-like example and to witness to those who used to make me feel like nothing.

—NATHANIEL

Persecution can provoke to live at a higher level.

My friend and I started a Bible club at school. We started with seven people, but in 2000 after an Acquire the Fire event, we had about 200 people. We had outreached at the school's Quad, and people would come to know Jesus even though others laughed or did not care.

After a shooting at our high school we began to pray at the Quad every Monday. At first people would not even look at us. But then as we continued to pray people gathered, and we ended up with more than 200 teenagers on the circle. In memory of that prayer a tree was planted at the place where we prayed. My teachers and friends wanted to know about Jesus because of what they saw.

During my senior year I was faced with so much persecution. In my economics class I had to sit by these gothic guys who made fun of my beliefs all the time. On Halloween one guy dressed up like Satan and said, "Look, I'm Jesus." I never answered badly to them. I always ignored them even though my heart ached for their salvation. All my classmates would watch my reactions. Around November, I invited them to see "Heaven's Gates and Hells

Flames," and although they didn't go, one of their friends went, responded to the altar call, and asked Jesus into his heart. His life was totally changed. He talked to his friends about God, and he would try to stop them when they made fun of me. By the end of the year the rest of the class wrote messages on my yearbook saying that they admired my Christ–like character.

At junior college I kept praying for the gothic guys' salvation, and one sat by me in English class. One day God put in my heart to talk to him about Jesus. He listened this time, and he never made fun of me again. He would even ask me about church. He was different, and when he was going through rough times I told him I would pray for him. I know I planted and watered the seed in their lives, and that one day it will grow. I always had the joy of the Lord even though I was persecuted.

—LUZ

Be prepared (especially in times of crisis) when people are looking for someone who will stand up and lead them.

26

"Who will help me fight against the wicked? Who will stand with me against those who do evil?"

—*PSALM 94:16*

In this verse God's heart cries out for someone to stand up for Him against the wicked. It seems like the wicked are always having more fun, they are always more popular, and they always have their "act" together. Today God's eyes look to and fro looking for someone who will have a backbone. Today is going to be your day to seize every opportunity you can to be that person who will stand for Him against the world that loves to do evil.

27

School administrators told my Bible club we couldn't put up posters. We couldn't pass out God's Word. So I studied up on it in Jay Sekulow's book about rights on campus, and I had a meeting with my principal. He couldn't say no, because I knew my rights. When I was able to share those with others, we were bolder about preaching in our classes.

I've since had opportunities to read my Bible to my class, talk about salvation, get out of assignments that contradicted God, and witness to a nice group of teachers. Our club also prayed with teachers and cleaned up their classrooms. When we prayed with one teacher with a bad back she was healed. God is good!

Honestly, it felt great. I was able to defend my faith, and I knew what I was talking about. God put a desire in my heart, and I researched it so I would be prepared. I was so excited to find out all the things we could actually do on campus and that lawyer Jay Sekulow defends court cases of Christian teens who stand up for their faith on campus. I was also given the privilege to encourage so many other Christians on my campus to also stand up.

"When you are arrested, don't worry about what to say or how to say it. At that time you will be given the things to say. It will not really be you speaking but the Spirit of your Father speaking through you" (Matthew 10:19–20).

"God did not give us a spirit that makes us afraid, but a spirit of power and love and self–control" (2 Timothy 1:7).

—RACHEL

29

Don't let anyone throw cold water on your fire. If you know the law you can stand up boldly.

Jay Alan Sekulow, "Students' Rights in the Public Schools" *www.aclj.org*

I have been made fun of for being a Christian since my sophomore year of high school. It wasn't so bad at first, and then it got worse as my boldness for Christ increased. Our prayer circle was being called the "God Squad," and kids in class were making fun of me. Through all that I was still able to keep strong. I even tried to help those who made fun of me. I don't know if I made an impact on the worst of them, but the ones who were less hostile came to respect me and my faith.

Also, someone who is now one of my good friends saw me reading my Bible late one night. He kept asking why I was reading, and I said I needed to find answers. Later I learned that my friend said the main reason he became a Christian was that night when I was looking for answers to my questions in God's Word. My friend is now a strong Christian; he helps out his youth group, and his life has been completely changed by Jesus Christ. All of this happened from one moment in time when I was getting closer to God.

Being made fun of has taught me a lot about patience; I stuck around a group of kids because I was searching for an opportunity to witness to them. It helped me to see that just because these teens are deep in sin I shouldn't shun them. God can turn anyone around at any point in their life. I was there to help plant seeds for God, and I did whatever I could to be an example to them. I wanted to be able to help them, and even though they didn't know it, I would always help them if they asked.

—JUSTIN

Many times it's the little things that affect people the most.

The summer before my senior year of high school, I gave my life to the Lord, turning away from a reputation as a "partier." I refused to let this change go unseen by my classmates and teachers. I also thirsted to pray for my school daily. A group of Christian friends decided to pray for everyone who entered the school each morning. We sat near the doors and prayed for each student and teacher who entered. I cannot even begin to count the comments and insults that were hurled at us daily.

I felt like quitting the prayer group. I was searching for a reason to quit, a reason from God. But, the more I looked for that reason, I found MORE reason to continue the group! So, I pressed on. People accused us of being members of a cult; we were told that prayer is not allowed in school; people would bring up accusations of their rights being violated because of our prayers. Those are exactly the attitudes that fueled our desires to pray.

I realized that my reward IS NOT ON EARTH. What I was doing was so much greater than anything here on earth. I was fighting an unseen battle, and because of what I did that year, I see that oftentimes the battles that I fight are on my knees. I understand that now.

—KRYSTAL

Persecution ought to strengthen our decision to follow Christ, not weaken it.

WHEN PEOPLE INSULT YOU BECAUSE YOU FOLLOW CHRIST, **YOU ARE BLESSED,** BECAUSE THE GLORIOUS SPIRIT, **THE SPIRIT OF GOD, IS WITH YOU.**

—1 PETER 4:14

33

I have so many non–Christian friends who needed to know what God did in my life after an Acquire the Fire event. I had to tell someone! After school I started sharing with a friend what God had done. She was a committed Mormon, but I had to tell her. After about two days when I was reading my *Extreme for Jesus Promise Book* and telling her this awesome thing I was reading she simply said, "Shut up." She said people were tired of my talking about God, and that I was making them angry. I asked her how I could make people mad about my own experience with God, she couldn't answer that one. I kept praying for her daily, because God wants her in His kingdom.

So often in church we are told that once you accept Christ it's an easy ride, but it's not. I have been made fun of many times for wearing Christian shirts. My nickname from friends became "church girl." It hurt so badly when someone I thought of as a friend hurt me. I already felt so unsure about this newfound joy I had; how could someone completely disregard it? But I just asked God what to say, and His answer was silence. That's all I could do: turn the other cheek to the insults. I was happy to be made fun of as long as they realized that I serve someone better than me, better than this world. It can be such a humbling experience. People are going to try to hurt you, try to get you down, but your roots are deep and others have nothing on you. I tell everyone my story, the story of Jesus. Why hide it anymore? Everyone deserves to hear the story. Our God was persecuted, so how can we hide in shame when we are, too? We feel that God abandoned us, but He wants us to tell more people. I can't be silent about that! I should have realized that all along.

35

Why let these people pass us day after day and them not know a thing? It's not for the glory of us but the glory of God. I felt so unsure of what might happen, but God doesn't call the qualified, He qualifies the called—and He qualified me. Why not use that to help plant seeds on my high school campus?

—MALLOREE

"Blessed are those who are persecuted for righteousness' sake, for theirs is the kingdom of heaven" (Matthew 5:10, NKJV). We should be happy to be made fun of!

I am a Christian. When people talked behind my back, made fun of me, or threw garbage at me, its purpose was to slow me down spiritually, but it sped me up and I pursued the Cross even stronger. Some of those who persecuted me later came to me for prayer when they needed it. One day, I was eating lunch with my friends when a girl came out of the bathroom holding her stomach and walking slowly. My friend asked her what was the matter, and she replied that she had been sick and that she was on her way to call her parents to pick her up. Now, the bolder you are with people, the bolder God will be with them, so I asked her, "Do you want to be healed right now?"

She said yes, so I asked her if I could pray for her. She agreed, so we sat down. I explained that I wouldn't heal her, but that it would be Jesus and she wouldn't feel sick anymore if she believed that Jesus could heal her. Five minutes after we prayed, she said, "I went to the office and picked up the phone and realized I wasn't sick anymore. So, I am going back to class!" Praise God He healed her!

The next day I was talking to a Hindu girl who was there when I prayed the day before.

She had seen the girl come back healed. Her stomach hurt and she wanted me to pray for her, too. So I first explained to her Jesus is the One who heals and that He came to earth, died for us, and rose again. When I went to pray for her she sat down in the same place the other girl sat (she must have thought it was the "hot seat") and Jesus completely healed her that second! Glory to God!

I learned to never give up, to keep on keeping on because "He who is in [me] is greater than he who is in the world" (1 John 4:4). God will always be there, so I learned to never quit. I do it because He did it for me. He was persecuted yet He healed the sick; He was crucified, yet He saved us; He rose from the dead and is living in me. Why should I stay silent when the living God is in me?

—HAIFA

Jesus is the source of ALL healing—physical and spiritual.

I was in charge of organizing the "See You at the Pole" rally at my high school all four years. The first year I was the only one at the flagpole. When the school buses pulled in, the kids would scream profane things and laugh at me. I was embarrassed and nervous, but I kept pressing into God. Each year more Christians would come, but more laughing and mockery still came when the buses arrived. Most of the people who laughed were my so-called friends and other people I grew up with. Every year when "See you at the Pole" came I would pray for the people in my school, and each year the laughter grew. I wanted to see my high school changed, and one way I knew to do that was through praying.

At my first year of community college I went to "See You at the Pole," and as I walked up two guys and one girl ran up to me. I had known them since grade school, and they had been among the ones laughing and mocking. They told me how Jesus had changed their lives, and they were at "See You at the Pole" for the fifth year in a row—this time to PRAY! Since then, one gentleman is studying for his pastoral degree, and the other gentleman and lady are seeking the Lord together in their marriage.

—KRISTEN

Persevering in your faith against popular opinion sends a strong message to those who mock you.

39

STAND UP! I HAVE CHOSEN YOU TO BE MY SERVANT AND MY WITNESS—YOU WILL TELL PEOPLE THE THINGS THAT YOU HAVE SEEN AND THE THINGS THAT I WILL SHOW YOU.

—ACTS 26:16

I used to be as timid as a squirrel in front of a semi, but after an Acquire the Fire rally I saw through a lot of that. I got home and was so on fire for God that a friend and I took all our secular CDs out behind his house and shot them with his rifle. It was the greatest feeling! The next day at school the word had gotten around about we had done. Nobody seemed to understand. I felt somewhat alone at first. I was very hesitant, and then I just jumped off the cliff and told everyone that I had indeed shot my CDs. "What?! Why didn't you just give them to me? Are you stupid?" they said.

However, I kept thinking to myself, "I can't back down now!" We explained to them our views and our heart to change in hopes that they'd understand. They kept after me about it for about one class period and that was that. This wasn't necessarily a blatant act of harassment or anything like that, because it was basically my friends who were teasing me about it.

I learned that it's okay to be different, and my friends eventually decided what I was doing was pretty cool. I had had all these horrible pictures in my head of being so lonely and unpopular if people knew I was a Christian; I had thought it might take away what little amount of comfort and friendship I had managed to gain over those couple years in high school. Little did I know that Christianity, "true" Christianity, was the only thing that BROUGHT those things! I don't know how much of my actions rubbed off on my classmates, but I do know that I have no regrets for doing what I did. And that in itself is worth more than all the CDs in the world.

—TODD

Music defines most teens' identity. When you make a stand like this it makes it very clear you no longer belong to this "group". You have found your identity in Someone Else.

41

I had a friend in high school who loved God and would share his faith every chance he got. His name was Matthew; he was an ordinary guy with a lot of zeal. He constantly received ridicule from people he would share his faith with, and even from some of his Christian friends. Matthew wasn't perfect, but his hunger to know God was awesome. At the beginning of his senior year, he did some things contradictory to his character, and those actions followed him. Given that he took such a bold stand for Jesus, people wouldn't let him live it down for weeks. The word "hypocrite" rang loud. Matthew had fixed his character flaws and was running hard after God, but people would still put him down and make fun of him for the stand he took.

At school Matthew attended a "See You at the Pole" rally with about 150 of the other Christian students. After the rally we interviewed him on video tape, asking him what he thought about the rally. He told us that God was going to do something amazing at the school, God was going to change students' hearts, and people were going to recognize their sin and turn from it by the hundreds. Matthew's heart was for the people in his school and for the local pastors to be unified.

After a worship practice at church that weekend, Matthew was driving some friends home and was killed in a car accident. We held a service for him on Monday and showed the video tape of him from the "See You at the Pole" rally, crying out to his school. God used that to change the hearts of the young people in his school, and 300 kids gave their lives away to Jesus. That was the most powerful altar call I have ever witnessed. I was encouraged that no matter what people said, Matthew stood strong and gained respect because of his courage, and as a result souls were won. His youth group had around 85 regular youth coming, and at the next service there were almost 200. Today almost 300 regularly come to the youth group.

—JEREMY

Don't ever think that one person can't make a difference.

LORD, TEACH ME WHAT
YOU WANT ME TO DO,
**AND I WILL LIVE
BY YOUR TRUTH.**
TEACH ME TO RESPECT
YOU COMPLETELY. LORD,
MY GOD, **I WILL
PRAISE YOU
WITH ALL MY
HEART, AND I
WILL HONOR
YOUR NAME
FOREVER.**

—PSALM 86:11-12

44

here I was with two of my best friends in another country. We were sort of on a mission trip, although we really hadn't planned it that way. We didn't have to raise support or anything to go. It seemed like God just provided a way for us to get to this land far away. My two pals and I loved God with all of our hearts, and we were determined to follow Him no matter what. It turned out that the king in the country where we were set up huge gods, including a huge statue of himself, and said that at a certain time every day certain music would play and we would have to bow down to this statue.

It seemed like everybody was falling down and worshiping this god, even our own friends who said that they followed God, the true and living God, but it didn't matter to us. Even if everybody else bowed down, we weren't going to worship anything other than the true and living God. He had already given us favor and we had been promoted as leaders in the land even though we were there against our will— we had been taken there as prisoners along with thousands of others from our country.

There was no way we would worship a

piece of gold and bronze! We served a living God! The king didn't really notice that we weren't bowing down until some trouble—makers told him that the three guys whom he promoted wouldn't bow down and worship his god. The king was furious and he sent for us. He gave us one more chance to bow down and worship his god, and he said, "If you don't bow down this time you will at once be thrown into a flaming furnace, and no god can save you from it."

We just told him, "Your majesty, we don't need to defend ourselves. The God we worship can save us from your flaming furnace, but even if He doesn't we still won't worship your gods and the gold statue you set up." Boy, did that get him mad. He ordered all three of us to be thrown into the furnace and said that it was to be heated seven times hotter than usual. Then he commanded some of his strongest soldiers to tie us up and throw us into the flaming furnace. The king wanted it done at that very moment, so they tied us up and threw us into the flaming furnace with all of our clothes still on. The fire was so hot that some of the flames leaped out and killed the soldiers as they threw us in.

47

The strangest thing happened to us as we were thrown in. We knew that God could deliver us, but even if He didn't, that wouldn't change our minds. We were fully willing and ready to go and meet Him face–to–face at that moment. And we did meet Him there, though not the way we expected. As we entered the flames, instead of feeling a burning, searing sensation curling our flesh it felt more like a warm pool of water. We actually walked right into the furnace and walked around in it. Our ropes were burned off. We were free to talk to each other. Little did we expect what was about to happen. Jesus Himself came and spent time with us in that fiery furnace!

We were shocked to have Him greet us in what we thought was the end of our life and our utmost despair. It was so funny peering out and seeing how mad the king got when he looked in and saw that we were still walking around. We were high–fiving each other and talking about what a great conqueror our God is and how He's the only living God. We could hear screaming outside, but we didn't really care—we were with the Lord. Then we heard the king calling us, asking us to come back out of the fire. We really didn't want to go because we would have rather stayed with the Lord. But He said our job wasn't done yet.

Something must have happened to the king because he was shouting, calling our names and saying, "Servants of the Most High God come out at once." As soon as we came out the king started praising God for sending an angel to rescue us and take care of us. He was amazed that we would rather die than worship any god other than our own. So then he made a law that no people in his whole kingdom were allowed to worship any other god or say anything against our God or they would die. I just knew our God would come through for us. I just wasn't sure how He would do it, but I knew He always does.

—SHAD

TAKEN FROM DANIEL 3:1-29

Armed with the confidence that our God can deliver us—and the determination that even if He doesn't, it won't change our mind—we have boldness even when the rest of the crowd is following the wrong path.

I can still remember how sad I was at age eight when my dad died. My mom and others rushed around me trying to comfort me. The next few days I can barely remember because it was such a flurry. People started treating me differently. They started dressing me in really nice clothes. They had a parade and put me in the front of a crowd, and everybody was cheering for me. But all I could think about was that I was never going to get to see my dad again. Somehow it dawned on me that they wanted to make me the leader of the whole country even though I was just a kid.

My mom kept raising me, but I was also surrounded by very wise men who seemed like they really knew God or something. They kept telling me about what the Scriptures said and what God really wanted for the country and for my life. Finally, when I was about sixteen years old, it all came alive to me. I realized that God is really real and for some reason He had placed me on this earth to be a leader. I looked around and saw that people in my city and my country weren't following God, and even the church had been destroyed. I decided to use some of my authority; I told the leaders to clean up and remodel the temple so people could come and worship the Lord.

Soon after they started the work they began to find things that had been lost for a long time. They found Scriptures and scrolls telling all of the desires God had about how He wanted us to live. They read them to me, and I just began to weep. I couldn't believe it! We were supposedly a nation that "follows God," but we hadn't heard these Scriptures for years. The only thing worse than a bunch of people who don't follow God, is a bunch of people who say they follow God because they live in a "godly nation" but in their heart they really don't follow God—and that is what my nation was.

As soon as I heard these Scriptures, I called a big gathering. I asked everyone in the whole nation to come and hear God's laws. As I sent messengers all over the country to different towns to announce this, some people mocked and laughed, "What is this leader trying to do to us?" They acted like they didn't need the Word, but you could tell by the way they were living that they didn't know what the Scriptures said.

Thousands of people came from cities and towns all over, and we sat for a whole day and

read through all of the Scriptures. People
began to weep and seek forgiveness. We all
committed to get rid of everything else that
was worship to anyone except to God Himself.
Everyone who listened got so excited. We
began to take every idol, every statue that was
set up, every pole that had carvings on it, and
we began to smash them, cut them up, destroy
them, and throw them away. Some people
started getting mad at us. After all, they had
grown used to this stuff; even though they said
they worshiped God, they still loved all these
other things. I expected that a lot of people
would be angry at me for doing this, but I
knew that God had put me in this position for
a reason. I had to do what I knew was right.

—JOSIAH
TAKEN FROM 2 CHRONICLES 34:1–33

When we realize how God truly wants us
to live, He will require a drastic response
compared to the worlds standards. They
won't understand, but go for it anyway!

Have you ever felt alone? I have. I felt like I was the only one who still wanted to follow God with all of my heart. The strangest thing is that this loneliness came after one of the most amazing experiences of my life. I had just won out through a face–to–face encounter with a bunch of so–called spiritual people who were following false gods. They kept telling me I was wrong, so I said, "Let's see whose God is real."

We all went to the top of a mountain. They called all their religious people together and put together a big pile of wood and sacrificed a cow on top of it. They kept calling down their god to bring down fire and consume it. Of course, he never did. In fact, I had a little fun with it. I taunted them by saying, "Maybe he is sleeping or maybe he is going to the bathroom. Maybe that's why he is not coming down."

That just made them even madder. After hours and hours of that, I put together a pile of wood, sacrificed a cow, dug a pit around it, and put all kinds of water around it, and after just a short prayer the God of the universe came and consumed it with fire. It was amazing! I mean, fire came down out of heaven! People's hair got singed! It just took a moment. Immediately, we rounded up all of the leaders who were worshiping false gods, and they were all put to death. It was like the best sermon of my life! I was so excited that God had come through in such a powerful way.

Finally, now everyone could see that there was one true living God. No longer would I be persecuted, mocked or taunted...or so I thought. The king who was there went back and told his wife, Jezebel, about what had happened. Jezebel got really mad and said I would be dead by the next day.

I was afraid, so I ran for my life. In fact, I ran to another country because I was so scared. How could I run? How could I be scared? The God who created the whole universe just proved Himself, and suddenly I was running from a wicked lady who for some reason still didn't believe in His power. I felt stupid for being afraid, but I was afraid. I went to a hideout in the middle of nowhere. I said, "Lord, I've had enough. Take my life. I'm no better than anybody else." I then fell asleep under a tree.

An angel came and touched me. He told

me to get up, and he even brought some food for me and cooked it. I got up and ate and drank. It gave me strength, and I traveled for about forty days when I found a cave and spent the night. The Lord spoke to me, "What are you doing here, Elijah?"

I told Him: "I have been very excited about You, O God, but everybody turned their back on You. They have killed all the preachers in town. Now I'm the only one left, and they are trying to kill me, too."

The Lord told me, "Go back to where you came, and stand up for Me. Don't worry, I've still got seven thousand people whose knees have not bowed down to the false gods. They still love Me with all of their heart. Don't worry, you're not alone."

—ELIJAH
TAKEN FROM I KINGS 18 & 19

Even when you think you're the only one who still wants to serve God with all of your heart, be encouraged. God has many others who refuse to bow just like you.

No one ever looked up to me. In fact, I was the youngest one in my family. We were the weirdest people in my neighborhood, I was picked on my whole life. My family and our whole city lived in fear of terrorists all the time. They had taken many people hostage and killed many other people, so now many of us were afraid to go out of the house. It seemed like no matter what we did these evil people continued to prevail against us.

One day I just cried out to God and said, "God where are all the miracles we heard about in the past, that our fathers and grandfathers told us about that You did?" I heard God speak back to me as clearly as I could hear a person.

He said, "Rise up in the strength you have and save your whole nation."

I thought I was hearing things. What strength do I have? I'm the youngest guy, the strangest guy in the whole city. In fact I was hiding out just in case invaders came. But God was telling me that I have strength and I could rise up and do something about it? He must have been talking about somebody else, so I asked Him to prove it.

I put a piece of fur on the ground and I said,

"God, if I wake up tomorrow and the fur is dry, but there is dew on the ground, I know that You want me to do it." I woke up the next day and it was just like that. Again, I asked Him, "Well, God, what about the next day if the fur is wet with dew and the ground is all dry?" And wouldn't You know the next day I woke up and the same thing. God wasn't backing down from my doubts.

My heart started to race; the God of the universe was actually speaking to me. He wanted to use me to do something amazing. I didn't know what to do, so I asked God. He told me to round up an army. I sent word all over inviting people to come and join together. We were not going to stand for this terrorism anymore. Thousands came, but we were still way outnumbered. We had about 32,000 and they had about 120,000. But God said we had too many people in our army. He said that if we defeated the enemy with so many people, then we would think that it was our own strength and tactics that saved us. So I asked the men, "How many of you are afraid to go to war?" To those who lifted their hands I said, "Great! You're free to go home."

I had about 10,000 left. But the Lord said,

"You still have too many. Have them all come down to the river and get a drink." God told me that those who scooped up the water with their hands should go home, but those who bent down and lapped up water like dogs were going to be the warriors. Wouldn't you know only 300 lapped like a dog? 300 against 120,000? There was no possible way! But God's ways are different than our ways.

He planned a night attack. We struck the first blows with shouts and praises to God and blasts on our trumpets. The hills blazed with the light from the torches God told us to carry. And wouldn't you know that the enemy began to freak out and run? They got all confused and began to kill each other. God used a little squeamish boy like me who was never popular or cool to deliver a whole nation.

—GIDEON

TAKEN FROM JUDGES 6:1 – 7:22

It doesn't matter what you look like on the outside; when God looks at you He sees somebody He wants to use—if you dare to stand up and go for it.

God visits in both trial and in consolation. I have found when I lay down my life, not as a sacrifice to please others or myself, but as a sacrifice unto the Lord, a deep peace can reside in the midst of any storm. I Peter 5:7 says, "Cast all your anxiety on him because he cares for you" (NIV).

Thomas Merton said, "True happiness is to please Him."

Grace and peace to you,

PETER FURLER
NEWSBOYS

"I thought you were my best friend?"

STANDING UP TO YOUR FRIENDS

"But we are not those turn back and are lost.
We are people who have faith and are saved."

—*HEBREWS 10:39*

When persecution hits, it's easy for us to
think that we should just turn back. It seems
like it is just too hard to be a Christian. But
then we read that Paul exhorts us to remind
ourselves of the kind of Christian we are
committed to becoming. We refuse to let
anything provoke us to slow down in our
pursuing God and standing up for what's right.

hen I was in sixth grade, I got teased because a girl was cussing at me and wanting to fight, but I didn't cuss back. My so–called "friends" were laughing at me and telling me I was stupid because I didn't fight back. At first I was unsure of what I was doing, but immediately faith just surged into my heart. I told them very strongly that as a Christian who believed in Jesus, I wasn't going to cuss, and I didn't care that the girl had offended me—I wasn't going to offend God by talking back in the same way. As I was saying this I feared their reaction, but I knew deep inside I had made the right choice not to give in to the negative peer pressure.

I learned that everyone who hangs around you is not necessarily your friend. Friends are not the ones who just hang around for the laughs and good times, but true friends are there through the times when you're not the most popular person to be around. My real friends were the ones who stood by me when I held strong to my convictions. It was a BIG lesson to learn. I think back now on that painful decision and know it was the best decision I have ever made. That experience set a foundation for me, and I made a commitment that day to stand for Jesus. I set a public standard in my life to follow Christ in EVERYTHING I did, not just in private at home and at church, but at school, too. It was an awesome milestone for me. I learned I could trust God for every need, no matter how simple it was.

— CLAUDIA

_____

"You are the salt of the earth. But if the salt loses its salty taste, it cannot be made salty again. It is good for nothing, except to be thrown out and walked on" (Matthew 5:13).

When we act differently than the world expects we are truly salty. When we act like they do, we prove we have lost our flavor.

I remember vividly the week after I found God. I was so excited by the change in my heart and life that I ran full speed into my English class screaming "I found God!! I found Jesus!" The stares I received, the laughter I heard was a defeat in itself, but the greater loss to my spirit was yet to come. After my epiphany of the divine I raced up to my best friend to inform him, without much wisdom or tact, of the good news.

He looked at me as if he had never known who I was, a heartbreak that nearly caused me to lose my faith in that moment. In response to his constant criticism I decided to quiet down and share Jesus practically through a lifestyle rather than words. To this day I have found one thing to be true: despite the taunting, despite the laughter, despite the ridicule, in times of need my best friends have never asked anyone but me for advice, direction, and genuine God–given Love.

— T Y

Ultimately we must all ask the question whose opinion is more important? Our friend's opinion or God's?

The only temptation that has come to you is that which everyone else has. But you can trust God, who will not permit you to be tempted more than you can stand. But when you are tempted, he will also give you a way to escape so that you will be able to stand it.

—*I CORINTHIANS 10:13*

65

God constantly looks to give us strength to stand up. Sometimes we are called to stand when we are surrounded by temptation: our friends are saying one thing and asking us to do something, asking us to listen to an unhealthy CD, watch certain movies or act a wrong way. In the midst of that temptation God is looking for an army of people who will stand up. Be encouraged—He will give you the strength and the courage you need to take the stand in the midst of temptation to do the right thing. In doing the right thing you will be a light in a dark world.

O ne day, I heard the Lord speak to my heart. I knew that it was His voice because I had heard it before. He said, "Go over and speak directly to the King of Judah."

I was thinking, "I have to go over and speak to the king?"

Then He told me what to tell him. "Listen to this message from the Lord, you King of Judah, sitting on David's throne, then all of the other people will listen, too. This is what the Lord says: 'Be fair minded and just. Do what is right; help those who have been robbed, rescue them from their oppressors. Quit your evil deeds; do not mistreat foreigners or consume widows, stop murdering the innocent! If you obey Me, there will always be a descendant of David sitting on the throne here in Jerusalem. But if you refuse to pay attention to this warning, I swear by My own Name that this palace will become a pile of rubble.'"

I could not believe that God wanted me to say that to the king. Did He not realize what could happen to me if I told the king some bad news like that? Then God finished His message. He told me to tell the king: "Your family will not weep when you die if you disobey the Lord; your subjects will not even care that you died. You will be buried like a dead donkey dragged out of Jerusalem and dumped outside of the gate. When you were prosperous, I warned you, but you replied, 'Do not bother me!' Since your childhood you have been that way. You simply would not listen. Now all of your friends have been taken away as captives. Surely at last, you will see your wickedness and be ashamed. It may be nice to live in a beautiful palace, but soon you will cry and groan in anguish, anguish like that of a woman about to give birth."

Now I understand why God said to me at the beginning not to be afraid because He was going to ask me to do some things that outwardly seemed pretty scary.

—JEREMIAH

TAKEN FROM JEREMIAH 22:1–23

It's in these moments Jesus promises to never leave you or forsake you.

"Surely, those who love me most will understand!"

STANDING UP AT HOME

Driving into my driveway that afternoon I could tell that something was going on. As I got out of my car and walked up to the front of my house, I saw all of my belongings piled in front of the door on the porch. I couldn't imagine what was happening. I was 16 years old and had gotten completely turned on to Jesus just few weeks earlier. My life had been drastically changed. I immediately quit drinking, quit partying, and my life had done a 180 degree turnaround.

I tried to go inside, but the door was locked. This was strange because we never locked the door out in rural California. As I knocked on the door and waited, I wondered what could be happening.

The few weeks prior had been the most

dramatic of my life so far on this planet. I had been the most rebellious teenager a parent could imagine. Defying my father, insisting on my own way, out late nights all the time, but then Jesus totally changed my life. I continued to wait and wait for someone to answer the door. I had just returned home from high school and was planning to go to my job later that day. Finally, my younger brother came to the door. I asked him, "Hey Bro, what's going on? How come the door is locked? Why is all of my stuff out on the porch?"

70

I remember my brother, who up to that time was pretty much my best friend (because we have only thirteen months between us in age, we had done just about everything together) looked at me and said, "Dad said you have to leave."

I said, "What are you talking about?"

"Yeah, Mom said that either you had to leave or she was going to leave." He continued. "Dad chose you."

The 'mom' was my stepmother, who was only 26 at the time. I had lived with my father

less than a year when kicked me out. I grew
up with my mother until I was 15, when I ran
away to find my dad. We had had our ups and
downs, and I certainly didn't get along with my
stepmother very well, but I couldn't imagine
that it had come to this.

I said, "What do you mean I have to leave?
Where am I gonna go?"

He said, "I don't know. You just have
to leave."

I said, "Well, why?"

My brother replied, "Well, she thinks you
are too much into this Jesus stuff, and she
can't stand it anymore. You have to leave, and
I am not supposed to let you in the house."

It was a day I could never imagine
happening. I had no idea where I would go,
what I would do, how I would live, but I had
this feeling that God would take care of me.

Almost numb, I began to load my few
possessions from the front porch into my old
LaBamba–type of car. As I prepared to leave,
not knowing where I would go, I told myself

that somehow God would take care of me. I remember starting my car and driving out of the driveway praying with tears streaming down my face, "Lord, I have given my life to You trying to do the right thing, and now I've been kicked out of my house. Where am I going to go?"

I remember rummaging in the car for any spare money that I could use for food or lodging. As I looked in my glove compartment, there was a note from my brother and a five dollar bill. The note said, "Bro, I thought you could use this."

In that moment I began to realize no matter what the circumstance, God would take care of me. Somehow God always would get me through. As it turned out, God provided a place for me to stay with some college students from church. After a few weeks my pastor invited me to live with him, which was really a miracle because he had three teenage daughters. I lived with him most of my senior year.

We need to realize that when we commit our lives to the Lord, it may be that our family will have no idea how to respond to us and may even persecute us. But we can't let that hinder us or sway us from our conviction to follow our God no matter what.

—RON LUCE

"Those who love their father or mother more than they love me are not worthy to be my followers. Those who love their son or daughter more than they love me are not worthy to be my followers" (Matthew 10:37).

73

I AM PROUD OF THE GOOD NEWS,

BECAUSE IT IS THE POWER GOD USES **TO SAVE EVERYONE WHO BELIEVES.**

—ROMANS 1:16

74

I heard a story about a girl who after she became a Christian, her family turned their backs on her because they thought it was a cult. Her boyfriend broke up with her, and her friends didn't want to hang out with her anymore. She went to a youth meeting and was crying, asking the leaders if they would pray for her. She felt that something was wrong because she thought that this wasn't what was supposed to happen. Several of the youth leaders were praying for her. The head leader of the meeting came to her and said that he understood what was going on. He said it was good to pray when you lose everybody that was important to you for Jesus, but basically what it came down to was, "Welcome to the Cross."

I heard that story a couple of years back, and it radically changed the way that I think about the cost of walking with God. If you want to enjoy the blessing of the Cross you have to embrace the cost of the Cross.

—JOHN COOPER

SKILLET

75

My family and I have gone to church every Sunday of our lives. I always loved learning and applying everything our pastor would say, but my family seemed to just come and sit for a few hours. I couldn't ever express what I had learned each Sunday because they would toss in my face that I was judging them and telling them to pay attention in church. When discouragement comes from friends it hurts, but when it comes from family it causes deep wounds.

One day I said I had had enough of this lukewarm family, and I just started preaching to them. Telling them about the Word and about what it really means.

Being told to shut up about my faith from a "Christian" family only made me mad enough to keep doing it and keep doing it and keep doing it. One by one they each came to truly KNOW the Lord. They each have a passion for Him that was never there before. Now I KNOW my family will be in heaven with me.

—ANONYMOUS

ONE REASON
GOD PUT YOU IN
YOUR FAMILY IS
**TO REACH
THEM WITH
HIS LOVE.**
**DON'T
OVERLOOK
THEM** AS YOU
ARE TRYING TO
REACH THE WORLD.

"You won't need to fight in this battle. Just stand strong in your places, and you will see the Lord save you."

—*2 CHRONICLES 20:17*

78

This encouragement comes from the God who never abandons His children. He calls you to take up the battle, and He'll be right there with you. You are never standing up alone; He is always right there by your side. We're in the middle of the battle, you can't deny that. Our battle is not against the devil himself—that battle is God's alone—but against the souls of lost men and women.

As we stand up for our God, we take the battlefront right to the hearts of the people who see us standing up and are confronted with truth. Their hearts are pierced by seeing somebody with conviction who's not afraid to back down. Don't worry. Every time you stand strong, He promises to always be with you.

Walking into an enemy's palace with a stiff leg was not my idea of a good time, but for some reason it seemed like God was choosing me to deal with a tyrant who had been tormenting the people of God for years. I remember feeling since I was young that just maybe God had something huge for me, but I never dared to dream it could be something this big. There I was, just wanting to be used by God.

You see, this evil dictator had held our whole country hostage for seventeen years. Finally, people began to cry out to God, giving their hearts back to Him. Now God was ready to deliver us. You see, we had to pay a lot of gold and silver to this evil king every year. It was my turn to bring the payment to him, and I got this idea that maybe this is the moment that God would have me stand up and rescue my whole nation. So I strapped a foot–long dagger inside of my right thigh. Somehow I made it past security into the inner courts of the king's palace. I gave him the gifts, and as we were getting ready to leave I said, "Excuse me, king, I have a special message for you."

He told everyone to leave, so that we could be alone. Then I got close enough to whisper to him.

As I drew close I pulled the dagger from my right thigh with my left hand and thrust it into his belly. The king was a very hefty man, and as I let go of the dagger the handle disappeared into his belly and he fell over. I locked the door and escaped through the latrine while guards waited outside the other door.

I rounded up all of my friends and said, "Rise up! God has rescued us from this dictator." Finally, the guards busted in the door and realized their king was no longer alive. Now an entire nation was free to follow God and not a tyrant—all because God gave me the courage to kill a king.

—EHUD

TAKEN FROM JUDGES 3:12–30

God probably will never call you to kill a tyrant, but if he gave Ehud the courage to overcome one he can give you the courage to stand up against whatever ungodly circumstances are surrounding you.

BE ALERT.
CONTINUE
STRONG IN THE
FAITH. **HAVE
COURAGE,
AND BE
STRONG.**
DO EVERYTHING
IN LOVE.

—1 CORINTHIANS 16:13-14

"I'm going to do it even if I'm afraid."

STANDING UP WHEN IT'S PHYSICALLY DANGEROUS

Before the Soviet Union fell, I had the opportunity to go into the communist stronghold and bring Bibles to the people of that nation. We had been in a mission trip in Finland, and we were going to ride a bus with a bunch of Finnish tourists into the Soviet Union and bring Bibles, which were considered contraband. In fact any printed materials from the West: magazines, books and Christian literature, were all contraband. In other words, it was considered false publicity showing how great the West was.

I had heard stories of what happened to people who had been caught trying to sneak Bibles into the Soviet Union. I felt relatively confident, being an American citizen, that even if I was caught not much would happen, but who knew? This was a much–feared country with nuclear weapons while the Cold War was still going on. We had hidden the Christian literature carefully in our bags so that even if they did get searched, they might not be found. We also were bringing clothes and hard–to–find food items for the believers in the U.S.S.R.

At the border we began to go through

customs and immigration. One by one, Soviet
officers were studying people's faces. Some
rummaged through people's luggage. Some
people they ignored. When the officials got to
my bag, they opened it up and began to
search thoroughly. They found a Russian Bible
that I was bringing that I had written my name
in. You see, I had heard that it was okay to
take in your personal Bible. The Russian guard
pulled it out and looked at me and asked,
"What is this?"

"It's my Bible," I replied.

He said, "Can you read?" opening it up
and putting it in my face.

I said, "No, but . . ." and I opened the
very front and I said, ". . . it's my personal
Bible. My name's in it."

"You cannot read Russian Bible. It is not
your Bible. You cannot bring it."

I felt intimated at first, wondering what he
was going to do to me. Was he going to take
me to the back room? Then I just got mad. I
thought, "Why is this nation so intimated by a
book? What would make them pass laws to
keep the Word of God from coming in? It must

be that they know the truth will illuminate their darkness."

So I asked, "Why can I not have Russian Bible?"

He said, "You want Russian Bible, you go to Russia and buy Russian Bible."

I said, "Oh, I didn't know you could by Bibles in Russia."

He said, "Yes, you can."

So that sort of pacified me for a moment, but the anger didn't die. I had to take this Bible in, and I didn't want him to stop me, no matter what. So I looked right back at him and said, "Why? Why can I not bring this Bible to Russia?"

He looked at me with the darkness that I've only seen in the face of Russian soldiers, and I almost screamed.

"You do not ask WHY you cannot bring Bible into Russia. It is a RULE. That is why you cannot bring Bible into Russia."

He continued to rummage through our things. He didn't find anything else. Now the question was, what were they going to do with me and my three friends who were on our way into the country? We were on a bus full of tourists, and they didn't want to turn the whole tour bus around just because of us. They didn't want to leave us there alone, because then they wouldn't know what to do with us. So they decided to let us stay on the bus, just not with the things they had found. We got to St. Petersburg (which was then called Leningrad) and made our contact with the underground church, and we were still able to bring the other materials that they did not find into the former Soviet Union.

—RON LUCE

Something happens inside of you when you do not know or what might happen to you, but you know that you are standing up for what is right. There is a courage, a fire, a conviction, a perseverance that rises up in your heart knowing that: "It really doesn't matter what happens to me; I know that what I am doing is pleasing God."

If your enemy is hungry, feed him. If he is thirsty, give him a drink. Doing this will be like pouring burning coals on his head, and the LORD will reward you.

—PROVERBS 25:21-22

The Bible instructs us that when people are cruel to us, we must return kindness to them, and in doing so it will be like pouring burning coals on their heads. In other words, our kindness will begin to touch their hearts, because they had anticipated us to be angry or upset. When they experience kindness from us instead, the warmth of Jesus' love penetrates their hard hearts, drawing them towards Christ.

"When you are arrested, don't worry about what to say or how to say it. At that time you will be given the things to say. It will not really be you speaking but the Spirit of your Father speaking through you."

—*MATTHEW 10:19*

The way to prepare for any kind of persecution is making sure that your intimacy with Jesus is tight every day and that you are filling yourself with His Word. At the moment when physical harm may become a possibility, God will quicken what is stored up inside you and give you the right words to say. You can have great confidence and no fear in the face of whatever government authority, school authority, or non–Christian might try to hurl at you. It is right in the midst of persecution that words will flow from heaven through your mouth to pierce their hearts.

O n my flight home from a mission trip last summer, I met an amazing Chinese man in his seventies. He told me how in China he had been an editor for a major newspaper, but because he was a Christian and didn't agree with communism, he was imprisoned in a labor camp for twenty–one years. As he told me this, he never seemed sad. I wondered how he could so casually mention twenty–one years wasted. I asked him how he got through it so positively, and he told me that God was the One who got him through. He sang "Jesus Loves Me" and other songs. (That made sense; that's how I got through public high school.) I asked him what he did in labor camp; he said they did hard farming, but then he proudly told me that because of the labor he was still strong and healthy all these years later.

I was amazed. Rarely do you find a person who looks on the bright side of such things! After our talk I silently thanked God for letting me meet this man, and I determined that I would pray for my brothers and sisters who are persecuted for Christ "as though chained with them" (Hebrews 13:13, NKJV). Whether I am persecuted at home in America when people cuss at me for my faith, or whether a fellow Christian is persecuted in a distant land, in a way I am still persecuted. "If one part of the body suffers, all the other parts suffer with it" (1 Corinthians 12:26). I thank my God that He has shown me how to give thanks in everything.

—ALEXIS

Our troubles seem so overwhelming until we find a real hero of the faith.

I was in a country far away from home. The people there served all kinds of other gods, but it didn't deter me from having my quiet times. I'd pray every day, seeking God with all of my heart, even in a land full of people who thought I was a freak for it. I was the only one they knew who followed the living God with a real passion. Their mockery didn't deter me, but my strength made them mad.

Some people went to the king and attempted to make a law that said it was illegal to pray to any other god except to him, calling him the divine god himself. After this law was made, of course I kept having my quiet time, and the same people saw me through my window and reported me to the king. Well, the king and I had been friends. He had promoted me to a high position, but he didn't realize that people were just plotting against me. He had made a law and because it was the law of the land, he had to stick by it. So my enemies threw me into a den of lions, which was the sentence for anyone who defied the law. I didn't care. I knew that I might die, but it would be all the quicker that I could go and be with my Lord.

I wasn't sure what was going to happen there in the pit, but to everyone's amazement the lions just sat there and looked at me. They didn't approach me, and I certainly didn't approach them. I was up a lot of the night but then finally I fell asleep. When I woke up early in the morning I heard the king shouting my name, but it was still dark. As I opened my eyes I realized that one of the lions had actually come over and was lying next to me, and there was a big angel sitting with me, guarding me, making sure that I was safe all night. Wow! The king pulled me out of the pit, and I told him about the angel who had protected me all night. I said, "King, I have never done anything to hurt you or your kingdom."

He said, "Daniel, you were faithful. You served your God, and He was able to deliver you from the lions."

I said, "Yes, your majesty, I hope you live forever. My God knew I was innocent. He sent an angel to keep the lions from eating me.

He was relieved that I was rescued. Then he ordered the men who had been trying to get me in trouble to be thrown in the pit—the lions ripped them to pieces.

—DANIEL

TAKEN FROM DANIEL 6:1-24

It's the smallest things—the way you pray, the joy you have in your smile, or how you pray over your food—that irritate people and provoke them to try to harm you. You just keep following the Lord and doing what is right, and God will protect you.

93

"I can become like you any time I want, but you can never become a virgin again."

STANDING UP FOR PURITY

When I first got turned on to Jesus, I was 16 years old. I remember before then being the person who wanted to date every girl I could find who would say, "Yes." After I became a Christian not much of that changed. I just changed the reason for my going out. I thought, "Well, if I can find cute girls who need God, I can kind of minister to them." After a while I realized that probably wasn't such a good idea, so I would ask girls out who told me that they were "Christians." I was committed to the Lord and committed to living pure, and I figured that no matter what I did in dating situations, I wanted to make sure God would be pleased with it. Even though I really didn't know much about the Bible yet, I wanted to make Him happy.

I remember one girl who I went out with who told me she was a Christian. There we were sitting in the car and all of a sudden her quivering lips began heading in my direction. I began to fear for my life. I pushed myself all the way up against my car door as she continued to move closer. I was gasping for life and trying to talk some sense into her.

I kept pushing her away saying, "Wouldn't you rather be praying right now?"

She said, "No!" And she kept moving in.

I said, "Wouldn't you rather be reading your Bible right now?"

She said, "No, I wouldn't," and came right back at me.

I pushed her away again and said, "Are you sure wouldn't rather be praying?" (I just couldn't figure out any other way to bring up God in the situation, so I said the same thing again.)

She finally stopped and said, with an indignant voice, "No! Why? Would you?"

I said, "Well . . . yeah . . . I would rather be praying."

She said, "Well, I never!" And got out of the

car, slammed the door, and stalked off. I tried
to call for her and realized it was futile.

I realized this was the kind of response
that I inevitably was going to get by standing
up for what was pure. I later understood that I
shouldn't have been in that situation in the
first place. Thank God I had the power and the
strength to stand up for purity! But how much
easier would it have been if I would have been
in a well–lit place around a lot of other people
instead of alone in a car with a person of the
opposite sex? It is so much easier to stand up
for purity when you are not in an immediately
tempting situation.

— R O N   L U C E

Get ready for people to be offended and
slam the door in your face when they find
you standing for purity. They won't
understand it, but at least you will know
you are pleasing God and protecting your
future and your marriage.

"We have this treasure from God, but we are like clay jars that hold the treasure. This shows us that the great power is from God, not from us. We have troubles all around us, but we are not defeated. We do not know what to do, but we do not give up the hope of living. We are persecuted, but God does not leave us. We are hurt sometimes, but we are not destroyed."

—2 CORINTHIANS 4:7-9

After all the things that happened to Paul in the midst of all the persecution, this is essentially his assessment: "It's really not that bad. Sure, some bad things will happen to us, but don't worry. We're not giving up all hope."

It's important that amid persecution, as soon as you sense people's negative opinion, that you make a decision to say, "It just doesn't matter what they say or do to me, I will never give up. I am determined to stand. Things might be bad, but they could be a lot worse."

You can echo a determined and resolute Paul by saying, "It just doesn't matter what happens to me, I will never back down I will never compromise. Do to me what you may, I've chosen the way I'm going to live—and I will never change my mind!"

Throughout my life I had heard and seen Christians boldly stand up for their faith in God, and I wanted to be like that, too. One night at a youth group service a college student told us how he had been persecuted for his purity in the Lord when he didn't "check out" a pretty girl. When asked why he didn't, he said, "Because I want to keep my eyes pure for God." And I thought to myself, "Wow! I want to be just as BOLD as that!"

A couple of nights later I was at work and a pretty teenage girl walked in to buy some clothes. After the girl left, one of my co-workers came up to me and said, "Did you check that girl out? She was hot!"

I said, "No."

He laughed and asked, "Why?"

At first I hesitated with my words but then declared, "Because I want to keep my eyes pure for God."

He said, "Oh . . . you're a Christian . . . that's nice."

I had boldly stood up for something! It was so awesome! God was working through me and

He gave me the courage to say that! Jesus
is awesome!

—JOE

Make every action count. Be sure and tell
"why" you are doing good things, don't
just do them. "You should be a light for
other people. Live so that they will see
the good things you do and will praise your
Father in heaven" (Matthew 5:16).

101

THE EYE IS A LIGHT FOR THE BODY. IF YOUR EYES ARE GOOD, YOUR WHOLE BODY WILL BE FULL OF LIGHT.

—MATTHEW 6:22

All of my life, I have been the shy type. I never wanted to speak in public or in front of any sort of group. But last summer I went on my first Teen Mania mission trip, and my leader got right up in my face. He told me God was showing him that I was like Moses. God wanted me to stand up and speak, but I was hiding behind excuses that He should send someone else.

That conversation changed my whole life. Just saying, "I believe what I do because I grew up in the church" wasn't enough anymore. It made me question my faith. WHY do I believe this stuff? Is it really real? How does it hold up in life? And the answer to all of my questions became God. Yes, He is real. I believe this stuff because God made me and knows so much better than I do what is good. God can and will do anything through us if we just let Him.

This summer I went on a Teen Mania trip to Botswana, Africa. I was a leader, which was a challenge, but one ministry day in particular was especially challenging. We were giving AIDS talks in high schools. When I stood up and said I was a 21–year–old virgin, I was mocked to my face. A year ago, that would have been enough to send me running away in tears, but God gave me this supernatural compassion for the students and a boldness to speak the truth in love. For roughly forty–five minutes, I answered the questions of sixty curious teens. They continued to mock me, but as I stood my ground, they began to listen. I shared that my hope and strength come from Jesus.

That day just showed me how far we can come. I can't tell God that I can't or won't do anything, because I am no longer my own. Sure, maybe I am shy inside and don't have the words, but He can do all things through my life, as long as I yield to Him! Don't ever tell God He can't, because He can and will, if we just surrender!

—MICHELE

103

_____

Just because you have been told you are shy doesn't mean you are shy. "God did not give us a spirit that makes us afraid, but a spirit of power and love and self–control" (2 Timothy 1:7).

One time I felt very persecuted while I was in the choir practice room playing the piano and trying to write music. Some senior guys walked in and started talking about what they were going to do that weekend: drink alcohol, do drugs, and be promiscuous. I couldn't stand hearing them talk, but I tried to stay as calm as I could. Unintentionally, I rolled my eyes. They gave me strange looks. "Let me guess—you don't drink, or do drugs, and you're probably a virgin," one of the guys said.

I had two choices: I could stand up for God or I could not. I chose to stand up for Him. I replied confidently, "No, I don't, and yes, I am." From then on, every time I came into choir they harassed me and called me names like "virgin" or "high and mighty." I would not respond to them because I knew better. What did their opinion really matter? They graduated eventually, and I haven't seen those guys since. In the long run, they won't even remember me, but if they do I hope they will see me as someone who made good decisions. I really had to make a decision about what I believed and how important it was to me. I'm glad I chose to please God, whose opinion really matters. From that moment on I was a lot more bold about sharing my faith and a lot more firm in my convictions.

Their persecution made me more focused as a believer and more determined to win souls for Christ. I pursued God at a much more passionate level. I had made my choice, drawn a line in the sand, and that gave me confidence to demonstrate convictions that before I had only held tentatively. It renewed my passion for witnessing and made me understand how important our testimony really is to the world.

I stood up for God, because I knew He had given up everything for me. If He could give up heaven to die on the Cross, surely I could give up popularity to bring glory to His name. Temporary situations and opinions will fade, but I knew the stand I was taking would last past graduation.

—ROBYN

Decide now how you will respond when your moment comes—because it will come.

A s an eighteen-year-old woman, most people would think what I was about to do was stupid. I could be killed. Making this decision was the boldest thing I'd ever done in my life. Hardly anyone who did what I was about to do ever lived through it. I only made this decision because I felt compelled to. I had to! I couldn't just sit back and watch an enemy destroy my family and my friends. I had been encouraged by my uncle to make this decision, but it was still mine to make. No one could make it for me. Either I made this stand for my God or thousands of people could perish. I never dreamed that my life and my decisions could make such a big difference! Miraculously, God had put me in the right time at the right place, so that my decision was going to have a big impact either for life or for death.

You see, somehow the king had chosen me as his new queen. Out of thousands of ladies I was the one who was picked. Imagine that! But because of some shady guys trying to make some political move, all my family and friends were now in danger of death. How could it be that God would place me at just the right time and the right place to have such an amazing, significant impact? I knew how much was riding

106

Letters from the Bible

on me, but this was still the hardest decision I'd ever made—no one could go before the king, even his wife, unless they were invited.

As I appeared before the king, if he didn't extend his scepter, the guards would take me out and kill me. I walked through the door, knowing that if I died at least I would die doing what was right. As I entered the room uninvited, I closed my eyes for a moment. I opened them and saw the scepter was lifted. What a relief!

"What do you want, my dear Queen Esther?" The king said to me. I gratefully made my request.

Ultimately, the man who had schemed against me and my family was put to death instead and my people survived. Who would've thought that God could use a teenage girl to help so many people?

—ESTHER
TAKEN FROM ESTHER 4:1 – 7:10

The circumstances surrounding your life are not mere coincidence. The impact of your decisions to stand up could reach a lot of people.

"I'm choosing my God over my gift."

STANDING UP TO SPORTS PRESSURE

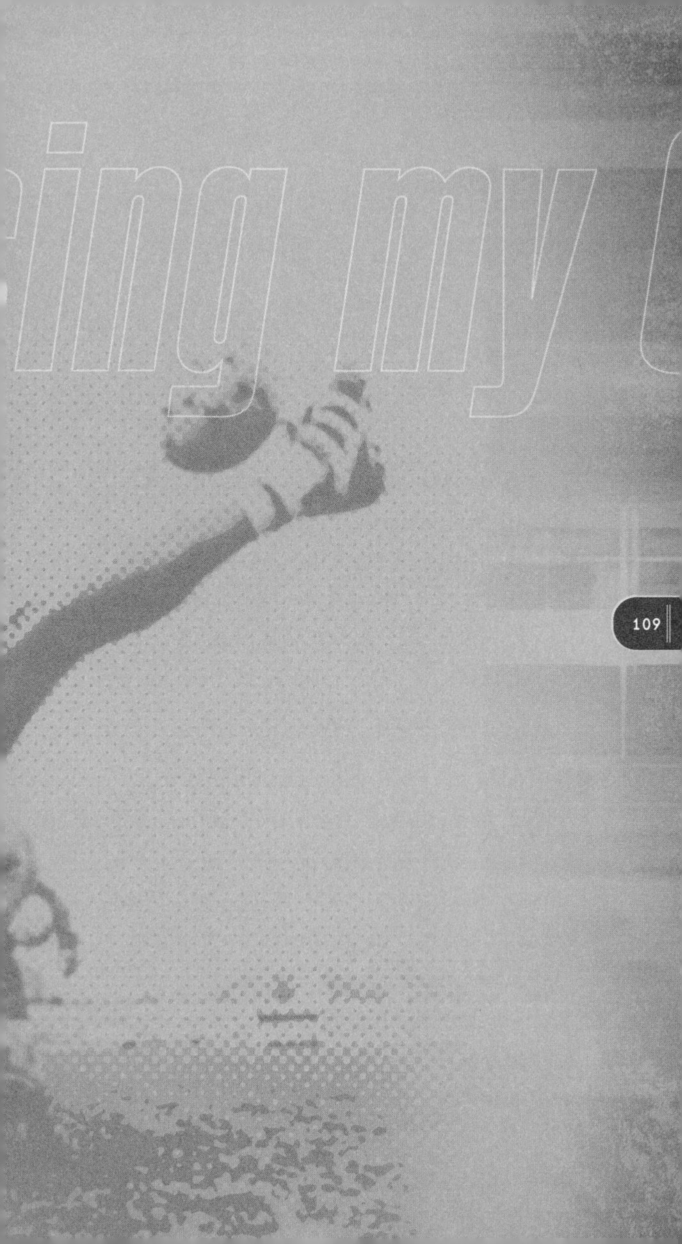
ing my

"No one will be able to defeat you all your life.
Just as I was with Moses, so I will be with you.
I will not leave you or forget you."

—*JOSHUA 1:5*

Joshua was up against formidable odds when it was time for him to take over the nation of Israel. He was the one leading the children of God. There were giants and huge armies in the land, but God promised Him, "As you stand up, don't worry; I'll be with you and I'll never forsake you."

Today you are leading a battle into your school, into your workplace, and you're taking the standard of God, the presence of God into some of the darkest places of the earth. Even though there may be giants there—formidable forces that look overwhelming—don't worry. You represent the living God, and He will not let you down. He will not fail to be right at your side.

As an athlete, it is very hard to be one hundred percent committed both to the sport and to God. I've played all my life, and in the beginning of high school a coach forced me to choose: soccer or God. This tore me inside because, of course, I love God, but I also loved soccer. I processed this all in my head in about two minutes. I had never realized how much precedence I was giving to soccer. So, I told my coach, "It's really hard to give up something I've *done* all my life, but I would do that before ever giving up my *way* of life."

I gave up soccer for God and stood up to the coach whom I had adored. God never gives up on His children. He knew what needed to be done in order for me to understand how important it is to be strong and bold, and Stand Up! Not just for what I believe, but for who I am.

Joshua 1:9 says, "Have I not commanded you? Be strong and of good courage, be not afraid, nor dismayed, for the LORD your God is with you wherever you go." This Scripture has revolutionized my life. I am constantly

111

meditating on this verse, and no matter what the situation, He tells me . . . "I am with you wherever you go." I have no reason to fear and every reason to believe. I stand up for myself and for what I believe in now; I don't let anyone walk over my faith.

Sacrificing soccer was everything I always needed, but had never understood. In that time I was able to realize where my priorities were, and how they needed to be. God helped me learn how to be active and still two hundred fifty percent committed to Him. That way when people ask me how I do it, I have an open window every time to witness to them and tell them I get my strength from God.

—REBECCA

Hard decisions like these will shape the course of your life and the impact you have for Jesus.

s far as I was concerned he was just another bully. I had dealt with bullies before and I wasn't afraid of this guy. As I ran with all of my might towards the bully, my eyes were studying the rocky ground for just the right weapon. It seemed like all of my brothers and friends were afraid to stand up to this guy, but somebody had to let him know that you can't mock my God and get away with it.

Even though I was sixteen years old, my God already had helped me with a bunch of other bullies. In fact, while hanging out in the wilderness, I had actually taken down a bear and a lion. This bully would be no different. I didn't feel like a hero or anything, I just knew that God was on our side. For weeks now this bully had been taunting the whole country. Our army stood paralyzed as he hurled every insult you could imagine our way.

I couldn't believe everybody just sat by and let him mock our God and our army week after week. Finally I went to our leader and said, "I'll go." Everyone began to laugh because I

113

was so young. Then I told them of the battles God already had helped me fight and win. They armed me with traditional war gear, but it was way too heavy. When I said that God would deliver us in another way they finally let me go. I grabbed my five perfect stones and looked the bully right in the eye. He called me a dog. Can you believe that?

I didn't really care about the personal insult, but his mockery of my God burned me. So I grabbed that first stone and hurled it his way with my slingshot. Bulls-eye on the bully! The rock hit right between his eyes and down he went. Everyone but me was surprised. Just to make sure he was dead I took his sword, cut off his head, and brought it back to the king, so he'd know for sure that this bully would no longer terrorize our neighborhood or mock our God.

All the other bullies I had defeated had prepared me for this big battle, because I had stood up courageously in smaller things. This just seemed like the next logical step. Little did I know that starting my teenage years by conquering giants like this would lead to a whole life of amazing partnership doing great feats with my God.

—DAVID

TAKEN FROM 1 SAMUEL 17:1—51

Courage in the small challenges will prepare you for the Goliaths that are to come.

HOW CAN A YOUNG PERSON LIVE A PURE LIFE? BY OBEYING YOUR WORD. WITH ALL MY HEART I TRY TO OBEY YOU. DON'T LET ME BREAK YOUR COMMANDS.

—PSALM 119:9—10

"My beliefs can withstand your disbelief"

STANDING UP IN MY CLASSROOM

I went to a secular graduate school where all of my classes were taught by non-Christian professors, and in all of my years of school there I only found one Christian classmate. My classes were all about counseling and psychology, and we supposedly were learning how to "help" people. In daily class discussions, whenever they would ask me for a comment I would, of course, refer to the Bible or a principle from Scripture or something God had done in my life.

Every day I was assaulted verbally for my beliefs. This being a college, my peers and teachers could get away with cussing at me, verbally abusing me, demoralizing me, and trying to humiliate me in front of everybody.

Had I not been confident in my faith I would have been in trouble. They said things like, "Are you a computer? Is all you can say from the Bible? Don't you have any real feelings?" On other occasions they would say, "You just use the Bible as a crutch because you can't make it in life." I knew that every day in class I would encounter some sort of punishment and abuse.

These people were very intelligent. Sometimes it was intimidating talking to people with doctorates about this God who changed my life. Sometimes they would bring up a point, and I wouldn't know what to say. I would go back and talk to friends who loved God, and I would pray and ask God, "Give me the words that will silence the mouths of really smart people." I knew that God is all wisdom and all knowledge and that He could blow away any argument no matter how smart the secular person might be, because He is the answer to life. Then I would march into class with confidence, knowing that God would give me the appropriate responses.

I would ask and ask and ask and ask God and strong Christian friends how they would respond, so that I could go back into class more prepared. It pushed me to explore my beliefs in a way that didn't make me just look like an airhead. When faced with challenges so many Christians say, "Well, I don't know," or "I just trust God," or "I just believe." It makes us look like we haven't thought deeply about what we believe.

The fact is even when we don't have the answers—yes, we have faith and we have great trust and confidence in our God—but when we don't have the answer, it ought to drive us to our knees in prayer. It ought to compel us to ask questions of people who are wiser than us, so that we become people who know how to account for what we believe. I thank God for the battery of questions and insults that I faced daily, because it refined my faith and my confidence in God and it forced me to become a "learned" Christian.

—RON LUCE

"Study to show thyself approved unto God" (2 Timothy 2:15, KJV).

During my sophomore year in high school, I had an English teacher who was extremely pessimistic. She didn't believe that God is good. One day, she said that God is bad and coldhearted. Coming from this teacher, who is HIGHLY respected in the school, the "Christians" in my class didn't say anything. However, I definitely don't tolerate ANYONE saying that about my God, especially not after all He's done for the world and for me. I had dealt with people acting like God wasn't real and all, but I couldn't believe what she was saying. I just felt this heat sensation throughout my body and knew that if I didn't say something, I would explode. I knew that it was the Holy Spirit.

I told her just how "bad" my God was. I reminded her that she had cancer when younger, yet she survived. "If my God is so 'bad' as you say, then why is it that He let you survive your cancer?" I've had a lot go wrong in my life, yet I don't dare call my Lord and Savior "coldhearted" or "bad." She brought up the story about Abraham, and how God told him to kill his son to see if he really loved Him and had faith. I told her that if God was so mean, then why didn't God let Abraham kill his son? You know, it's cool how when you have the Holy Spirit on your side, it doesn't matter what an unbeliever says, because the Holy Spirit will give you the words to say. After that I went to my locker and got my Bible out and went to show her the rest of the story directly from the Bible. She couldn't say anything; I had won the discussion. I had God on my side and who can argue with God when He's perfect?

Through it all, I felt God's presence and protection. It was as if I had a different type of power and was unafraid of what could happen with me saying what I did. God gave me the strength to stand up to my teacher and tell her what I needed to say. It's shown me that no matter what type of situation we are in, God is always protecting us. Feeling His presence all around me made me realize just how REAL He is.

—MINNELLIS

God will give you right words for the right time. "At that time the Holy Spirit will teach you what you must say" (Luke 12:12).

I gave my life to the Lord the week before starting eleventh grade. People in school knew me for doing drugs and other such stuff from the way that I was before becoming a Christian. That semester, I took a course where we debated a lot. I always defended my beliefs during these debates, but I was always put down or told to shut up. People said I was naive. However, I started many conversations and relationships and was able to share more of my faith; it was the only right thing to do. I had seen who God was and what He had done in my life, and so standing up was just something I had to do.

At times I felt like I was alone. It seemed like no one was listening to me and that I wasn't making any difference at all. I didn't always feel strong or have the answers, but eventually I started to trust more in the Lord's strength. I knew God had done a mighty work in my life, and that was something to declare. I became a stronger Christian because they were so hard on me. My heart was changed for them; my heart went out to them. And because my heart went out to those in my school, my heart also changed for my town.

The school persecution allowed me to experience something that I had never experienced before. I received a small taste of what other Christians around the world go though every day. I know that these experiences have made me more confident in who I am and what I believe in. I learned that I cannot do anything on my own strength, that the Lord will give me the strength to complete His will, and that I never have to be afraid of being alone and without an answer.

—PAUL

123

"Sometimes I say to myself, 'I will forget about the LORD. I will not speak anymore in his name.' But then his message becomes like a burning fire inside of me, and finally, I cannot hold it in" (Jeremiah 20:9).

I "came out" as a Christian when I was a sophomore in high school. I was trying to witness to my friend, and she was blown away by what I said. She began to mock me and was totally getting on me about my faith, thinking I was crazy. It made me feel small, but I knew what I was standing up for was right. Every blow to my faith made me stronger to take the next. It hurt, but at the same time I knew that it was worth it. It showed my friends that I was serious, that it wasn't just some phase, but I was willing to go through the ridiculing to share the secrets of this awesome life that Jesus offers. I also learned how to present the Gospel a little more gently.

I was driven by my desire for my friend to get saved. I kept praying for her, and amazingly she ended up signing my yearbook. She said she was totally inspired by my lifestyle. The next year I prayed and prayed for her salvation. Then one day I got another chance to share with her, and that week she came to the Lord!

Mark 13:13 says, "All people will hate you because follow me, but those people who keep their faith until the end will be saved." No matter what you face, keep pressing through! Though it might not seem that anything is happening, God is always working behind the scenes!

—COURTNEY

"We must not become tired of doing good" (Romans 6:9).

PRAISE THE LORD, GOD
OUR SAVIOR,
WHO HELPS US
EVERY DAY.

—PSALM 68:19

"Paul said, 'Friends . . . listen to my defense to you!'"

—ACTS 22:1

In this story, Paul has just caused a riot because he was standing up for Christ and preaching the gospel. Roman guards were taking him away so that he wouldn't get killed, but he insisted on standing up again and making even more clear the message of the Gospel he was proclaiming.

He did the exact opposite of what the "logical" thing might be to do. When most people would've quieted down just to get away safely, he insisted on speaking up. I want to encourage you to not necessarily do the "logical" thing. What seems logical in the natural mind might be opposite to what God really wants you to do in reaching out to the very people who are persecuting you.

Letters from the Bible

ord, You have persuaded me, and I know that I cannot change my mind. I shout, "Violence and destruction!" I tell the people that these are messages from the Lord—not foolishness for household jokes— and I cannot stop speaking what He has given me to say.

If I say that I will never mention the Lord or speak in Your name, Your word burns in me like a fire in my bones. I cannot hold it in! I have heard many rumors about me. They call me the man who lives in terror. I make everybody mad by the kinds of things I am saying to encourage people to live holy. They say, "He will trap himself." They say that they are going to get revenge on me. But Lord, You stand beside me like a great warrior.

—JEREMIAH
TAKEN FROM JEREMIAH 20:7-12

Let the conviction of doing what you know is right control your life, not other people's opinions. And you can be sure that the Lord will stand beside you like a great warrior.

"I'm living the life while I'm doing my job."

STANDING UP AT WORK

I got on fire for Jesus right before the summer between my junior and senior year of high school. I worked every summer on construction, and this would be a true test of my newfound faith. I was hanging out with my youth group a lot, but all day long, five or six days a week, I would be working.

Construction workers are notorious for telling bad jokes, sharing ungodly stories, and inventing new curse words. So there I was, in the middle of a bunch of guys like this every day working harder than most of them, yet at the same time unashamedly wearing my giant metal cross.

I would talk about the Lord whenever I could, but most of the times in the midst of the one hundred–degree weather beating down on my bare back, I was singing to the Lord. I mean all day long. Singing and working;

working and singing. I didn't care who was there, I would sing as loud as I could.

I remember singing, "Soon and very soon we are going to see the king."

One of the other guys on the job stopped and said, "Now what did you just sing?" I repeated the words. He said, "We are not going to see no king soon."

I said, "Oh yes we are!"

He asked, "What are you talking about?"

I said, "One day Jesus is going to come back. We are all going to see Him, and we are all going to bow the knee. The question is, are you going to go with Him when He comes or are you going to be left around?"

He just kind of laughed at me and said, "You're crazy. That's not going to happen."

I just kept on singing with all of my heart.

—RON LUCE

People may mock you when you first find your faith or when you first stand up for your faith, but eventually they see that you're serious. They see that Jesus has really changed your heart and changed your life, and they see that you are actually living the faith that you are talking about. They will find a different kind of respect for you, and then when they have questions or they can't figure out life, you are going to be the first one they come running to.

131

I DO NOT HIDE YOUR GOODNESS IN MY HEART; I SPEAK ABOUT YOUR LOYALTY AND SALVATION. I DO NOT HIDE YOUR LOVE AND TRUTH FROM THE PEOPLE IN THE GREAT MEETING.

—PSALM 40:10

"Then some Jewish people came from Antioch and Iconium and persuaded the people to turn against Paul. So they threw stones at him and dragged him out of town, thinking they had killed him. But the followers gathered around him, and he got up and went back into the town."

—ACTS 14:19-20

What an incredible legacy Paul gives us in this story! People intended to kill Paul because he preached the gospel. They threw stones at him until they thought he was dead. But that didn't discourage him. That didn't keep him from accomplishing his mission. He actually got right back up and went back into the same town determined to stand up for his God.

Let this example encourage all of us to refuse to quit. Paul refused to quit. The compassion of God overwhelmed his heart and

he went right back to the very people who drug
him out of town. He spoke, preached and
ministered to them once again. Ask God for
compassion right now to go back to the very
people who persecuted you the last time and
bring the love of God to them once again.

ne night at work, a co-worker asked me questions about what I believed. He told me he noticed there was something different about me and asked if I was a Christian. I told him that I was and he started questioning my faith. He is one of those people who makes fun of others and ridicules them for believing in God. He started asking me hard questions such as, "If God really existed then why were you born into the good family you were born into and I am stuck with a family that didn't teach me about God?" He also told me that nothing he'd tried—girls, drugs, alcohol, work, friends, family—filled the void in his life, but he wasn't sure if God was the answer.

At first I felt like giving up; then God changed my heart, and I enjoyed sharing my faith. I told him that "things" would never fill him, that nothing he tried could take the place of God, because we were created for Him. He actually thought that made sense, which surprised me because I thought he would just think I was crazy.

Over the next few weeks I took the time to

listen to his questions and attempt to answer them. Later he told me that at first he had tried to get me to question my faith, but when I didn't back down it made him think twice about the God I was serving. Before our conversations started, he had told me he would never go to church again, but after I got to know him better, he accepted my invitation to go to church. He actually loved it and wants to go all the time now. He told me that out of all the people he's ever known in his life, I was the ONLY person who ever took the time to listen to him and try to answer the questions to the truth he's been searching for. One day he said, "Sarah, I don't know why I was trying to change your faith and make you doubt, but it backfired on me. Now I believe! Thank you for being there for me to talk to and taking the time out of your day to listen and not judge me for the mistakes I've made."

—SARAH

Sincerely caring for those who mock you will prove the realness of the Love that has changed your life.

136

Once you have decided to follow Jesus, at that moment you have set yourself against every evil and ruler of darkness in this world, so it shouldn't be a surprise when you are persecuted. But as a child of God you can rest in His power to overcome whatever obstacle Satan throws your way. And remember that when you walk fearlessly through this dark world and continually trust in God, it is a sign to your enemies that your Father in heaven will save you. "God gave you the honor not only of believing in Christ but also of suffering for him, both of which bring glory to Christ" (Philippians 1:29).

RICK HEIL
SONICFLOOD

The Lord told me that even before I was standing up for Him and saying His words, my enemies were making plots against me. I was just like a lamb on its way onto the slaughter. I had no idea that they were planning to kill me. They hated me and the words that I shared. God said that they wanted to get rid of me once and for all. They threatened again and again that they would kill me if I did not stop speaking these words about God.

In fact, one time I was on my way out of Jerusalem and I was falsely arrested. They said that I was joining the enemy Babylonians. "It is not true!" I protested. But they were furious at me. They had me beaten with whips and imprisoned. I remained in this prison, which was more like a dungeon, for many days.

Later, King Zedekiah secretly requested to see me. "Do you have any messages from the Lord?" he asked.

"Yes, I do," I said. "You will be defeated by the king of Babylon." I could not believe what I was saying! Here I was in prison and I was telling the king that things were going to get worse. I did not care what he did to me; I knew that I had to speak what was true. Then I asked, "What crime have I committed? What

137

have I done against you or your officials and the people who put me in prison? Please do not send me back to the dungeon or I will die there."

So King Zedekiah let me stay imprisoned in the courtyard of his palace. Even while there, I kept telling the king and everyone who would listen that they needed to give their hearts back to God and follow Him, or the whole place would be destroyed. Some of the officials went to the king and said, "Sir, this man must die. That kind of talk undermines the morale of the few fighting men that we have left and all of the people, too. This man is a traitor."

King Zedekiah agreed: "Okay, do as you would like with him. I will do nothing to stop you."

Then they took me from my cell and lowered me by ropes into an empty pit in the prison yard. There was no water in the pit, but there was a thick layer of mud that I sank down into. I cannot remember how long I was down there, if it was days or weeks, but finally a guy from another country (who was an official serving in the palace) went to the king on my behalf. He said, "My lord, these men have done a great evil thing by putting Jeremiah the prophet in

138

the pit. He will die of hunger because nearly all of the bread in the city is gone." The king told him to take thirty men and pull me out of the pit.

But while I was in that pit, I called on Your Name, O Lord, and from the depths of that pit and You heard my plea. You came near to me and told me not to fear.

Thank You, Lord, for You have redeemed my life from the pit!

—JEREMIAH

TAKEN FROM JEREMIAH
37:11–21; 38:1–9 AND
LAMENTATIONS 3:52–60

It really does not matter the consequences. You can have great joy knowing that you have obeyed God, even if you are at the bottom of the pit, because you know that He will take care of you.

"But, you love God. Surely you will stand with me?"

STANDING UP IN YOUR YOUTH GROUP

One day in my quiet time I felt God speaking to me and telling me to go and stand in front of the temple and make an announcement to all of the people who were coming in and going out. He wanted me to say: "This is what the Lord says, 'If you will not listen to Me and obey the law that I have given you, since you do not listen to My servants the prophets whom I sent again and again and you would not listen to them, then I am going to destroy this temple."

All of the priests, prophets and people listened to me, but when I was done telling everything the Lord told me to say, the priests, prophets, and people at the temple mobbed me. "Kill him! Kill him!" they shouted. "Who do you think you are talking like that about the Lord's temple? What do you mean saying

Jerusalem will be destroyed?"

They thought nothing about their own sins, though, and the actual message about their lifestyle. All of the officials gathered in the city and they took me to the court. All of the leaders shouted, "This man should die! He is a traitor and prophesied against our own city!"

I spoke at my own defense: "The Lord sent me here to tell you what would happen to this city if you did not stop sinning and start obeying the Lord. The Lord gave me every word that I have spoken, but He will cancel this disaster that He has announced to you if you repent. As for me, I am helpless and in your power. Do with me whatever you think best, but if you kill me, rest assured that you will be killing an innocent man for it is absolutely true that the Lord sent me to speak every word that you have heard."

—JEREMIAH
TAKEN FROM JEREMIAH 26:1–15

Sometimes people who are pretending to be spiritual can be the hardest ones to stand up to and proclaim what is right.

little over two years ago the youth group that I attended was at the point when if ten people came it was a great success. However, those of us who did go didn't go to learn about God; we went to do our own thing. Then I got a wake–up call from God and completely turned my act around. God told me to tell the people in my youth group what had happened to me. I also told them that God said our youth group would double in size.

For a while after that I didn't see God move, none of my friends got saved, and I honestly felt doubtful. It was like, even though God had promised me that my friends would be saved, I still doubted it because I wasn't seeing anything happen. But something awesome during this period was that God gave me very clear, persistent dreams that made me more eager to pray for my friends.

In these dreams the devil would come into my school and hand out free food, and all my friends took it. After eating the food they would start to physically change, but none of them could see that it was bad. They all thought the changes were good and wanted more and more of the food. Only I knew that he was the devil and that the food wasn't good for them. I then shouted at him to get away from my friends, and he said that he didn't have to. As long as people wanted to eat the food he would give it to them. I then woke up and felt depressed, because the dream seemed to say that no matter what I did, the devil could still have access to my friends.

Because I was feeling discouraged I just opened my Bible and started to read Ezekiel 22. I am so convinced that God wanted me to wake up and read His word because Ezekiel 22:30 says, "So I sought for a man among them who would make a wall, and stand in the gap before Me on behalf of the land, that I should not destroy it; but I found no one." Wow! Did that put me in my place! After praying some more I fell asleep again and had the very same dream, but in the dream I walked and stood right between my friends and the devil. I rebuked him and told him that he had no place near my friends. He could not get through me because I was covered in the blood of Jesus, and he ran away!!! How awesome is that!

The next morning I was so energized. God had shown me that when I pray for my friends I am placing myself between them and the devil and that (in some ways) he could not get to them. I was standing in the gap. Because I took a stand many of the youth turned away from me, but I kept praying. Since then the devil has tried so hard to pull back what the Lord has been trying to do, but our youth group has grown to between forty and sixty people. We also have a separate night for Bible studies and prayer. I have seen more than twenty of my friends come to know God in a personal way, and many others have become interested in God. When I took my stand for God, even though God promised to change and save my friends, I couldn't imagine such a powerful outpouring. He is such an awesome God!

I also have learned to ask for forgiveness and say "I'm sorry" a lot. So many times I have had to be humble and ask for forgiveness for bad—mouthing my friends or being rude to them. I think this spoke to a lot of my friends the most, because not many people do that.

— M I I A

_____

When you stand up for what's right, the lukewarm youth group friends might persecute you. Just remember, it was the priests and religious leaders who mocked and persecuted Jesus.

146

"They are overwhelmed and defeated, but we march forward and win."

—*PSALM 20:8*

The people in the world who don't follow God are bound to fall on their knees. If you don't walk according to wisdom you'll always fall. When you don't base your life on the Word, your life is guaranteed to fall apart. This verse promises that we—as people who follow God with all our heart—will rise up and stand firm.

147

It seems exactly opposite of what we see with our natural eyes. Most of the time we see people of the world looking like they are getting stronger and stronger, while Christians look like we're losing the battle. But in this Scripture we can be confident that ultimately we will rise up and ultimately all others will fall. You cannot build your life on sin and know that it will stand.

I was born into a family where it seemed like everyone was into ministry—my father, all of my uncles, my grandfather—and at a very young age I thought, "Maybe God has something incredible for me to do!"

As I grew up, I just kept wondering, "Maybe God has something for me to do that would change this world."

One day in my quiet time the Lord spoke this to my heart: "I am your creator. Before you were born I chose you to speak for me to the nations."

I said back to him, "I am too young, and I'm not a good speaker, Lord."

I heard Him say back to me, as clear as I could hear a person speaking, "Don't say that you are too young! If I tell you to go and speak to someone then go! And when I tell you what to say, do not leave a word out. I will promise to always be with you so will not be afraid!"

Wow! Maybe God really had set me aside for something in His plan even though I felt young and inexperienced. He told me not to pay attention to my age and that He wanted to use me anyway. What could I say? Why was He telling me not to be afraid? Was I about to go into a dangerous situation? What would He want me to tell people anyway?

Then He spoke to me again. "I am sending you out with authority to speak to the nations for me. You will tell them of doom and destruction and of arising and building again." Well, no wonder He told me not to be afraid. I would have to tell people things they would not want to hear.

—JEREMIAH

TAKEN FROM JEREMIAH 1:1–10

149

God has an amazing plan for all of us. He put it together before we were even born but it is going to require boldness and no fear to stand up and have the full impact that He wants us to have.

I can't believe the amazing things that happened to me when I was seventeen years old. It was almost like I was in a movie or something. I was with my dad and about six hundred other guys. We were out in the wilderness having camp fires and talking about the good old times. These men were all tough guys. You could tell they had been outside a lot. They were all strong. They had actually fought in a lot of wars and had a lot of battle scars.

I was tagging along because my dad was a leader of this group and I just wanted to see what it was all about. I had loved God ever since I was small, and here were a bunch of men who also supposedly loved God as well. But I was about to discover that they didn't love God has much as I thought. You see, we had just come out of a battle shaped by a giant army that cornered us between these cliffs in the middle of nowhere. We had been waiting for days for them to leave so we could go home. No one knew what to do because we were outnumbered, so we kept waiting and waiting. Our food and water was running out and our enemies knew it; they figured we would either surrender or just die of starvation.

I couldn't believe that our guys were just sitting around talking and not doing anything to try to get us out of our predicament. Sure, things looked bad, but God was on our side, not their side. After all, we were His followers. Finally, I just couldn't stand it any longer. I couldn't just sit there and do nothing. Who did these enemies think they were? They weren't just fighting us; they were fighting the living God! So I decided to go up to the edge of the ridge and at least get a good look at the enemy. As I started off, my assistant came along. (I know it sounds strange for a teenager to have an assistant, except my dad was a leader in this group.)

He asked me, "Are you sure you want to do this?"

I said, "You bet I do. I want to go get a look at this ungodly army." Then I said, "Maybe God will act on our behalf. Maybe He will do an amazing miracle."

My assistant said, "Are you really sure about this? If you are, I'll go with you."

I said, "Well, I'm sure." So we went.

Just before we go to the top, my assistant said, "How do we know God is going to be with us or not? Maybe we will give our position away, and they will come kill us all."

I said, "I'll tell you what. If they see us come out and they come up and overwhelm us, we will know that this idea wasn't from God. But if the fear of God comes on them and they start running away, then we'll know that God is acting on our behalf and a miracle is happening." I know it sounded a little crazy, but I couldn't sit there and think that we were scared of a mere army when we had the God who created the universe on our side.

Up we went, and I stood at the top of the cliff and looked out. The army was massive. But then we heard them start screaming: "Look, the army of God is coming out of the rock! They are coming out of everywhere! Run for your life!"

Those guys began to run away. It was awesome! In fact, some of them ran over each other. Some of them killed each other. Tens of thousands of them actually fled for their lives, and many of them died on the way out. My assistant and I ran down after them, chasing

152

them away. Just the two of us! Well it wasn't long before my dad and his friends heard the commotion, and came up to see what was going on. They came running out, and we ended up chasing the enemies away. It really wasn't us, it was the hand of God working on our behalf. What a great day! I'll never forget it.

—JONATHAN
TAKEN FROM I SAMUEL 14:1—12

Many times the person who boldly stands up initiates a miracle from God. That one person causes the whole rest of the army or youth group to be bold. That one person can be you!

153

Conclusion

Conclusion

"Do I need to give more examples? I do not have
time to tell you about Gideon, Barak, Samson,
Jephthah, David, Samuel, and the prophets.
Through their faith they defeated kingdoms. They
did what was right, received God's promises, and
shut the mouths of lions. They stopped great
fires and were saved from being killed with
swords. They were weak, and yet were made
strong. They were powerful in battle and
defeated other armies. Women received their

dead relatives raised back to life. Others were tortured and refused to accept their freedom so they could be raised from the dead to a better life. Some were laughed at and beaten. Others were put in chains and thrown into prison. They were stoned to death, they were cut in half, and they were killed with swords. Some wore the skins of sheep and goats. They were poor, abused, and treated badly. The world was not good enough for them! They wandered in deserts and mountains, living in caves and holes in the earth. All these people are known for their faith, but none of them received what God had promised. God planned to give us something better so that they would be made perfect, but only together with us."

—*HEBREWS 11:32-40*

hen you see examples of heroes of the faith who endured such amazing persecution, it is hard not to be humbled. Some people have endured much greater hardships than any of us will ever know. It is encouraging to know that if they can endure their persecution, surely we can endure a little name–calling, a few confused faces, a little mockery for the sake of Christ.

Look at some of the things the heroes endured. They were put to death by the sword, mistreated, forced to wander in deserts and mountains, and even sawed in two. In fact, when you look at the extreme kinds of persecution that many of our forefathers endured, we have several reasons to rejoice.

First of all, we know we are in good company. If we are being persecuted for the sake of Christ, there are thousands of others who have endured the same thing for the sake of Christ. We're not the only ones. If they can do it, we can do it.

Secondly, you can look at whatever your situation is, no matter what is said or done, no matter how you feel, and then you can look in the mirror and say, "At least I'm not sawed in two." In other words, "It could have been a lot worse. Others have put up with a lot more for the sake of Christ than I have."

No matter how bad things might look right now, heroes who have gone before us have paid the ultimate price for their faith. Let us take courage from their examples. We can stand proudly, pull our shoulders back, hold our chin up high, and say that if they can face persecution with confidence, then how can we do any less than stand in humility for our God? After all He paid the ultimate price for us by giving His life.

Acknowledgements

This book is about real stories and real power, and Ron wishes to thank the real people who have shared their experiences to inspire and challenge all of us.

Many thanks also to Peter Furler of Newsboys, John Cooper of Skillet, and Rick Heil of Sonicflood for contributing to this book, as well as for their continued ministry through Christian music.

Thank you to the team at Teen Mania for working to raise up powerful young warriors for Christ: Bethany Englestad, Casey Wolston, Anna Osterdyk, Julie Sartor, Juliana Diaz.

And most of all, the Lord Jesus Christ deserves all the thanks and praise we can give. May we walk in His power every day.

About the Author

President and Founder Ron Luce started Teen Mania Ministries with his wife, Katie, in 1986. He has traveled to more than fifty countries, proclaiming the gospel of Jesus Christ. His dream is to empower young people to stand up for Christ in their schools and in the world. Ron meets with thousands of teenagers every week and would love to meet with you when he comes to your city. Call 1-800-299-TEEN (8336) or check out www.TeenMania.com to get in touch with him or learn more.

Teen Mania Ministries

Teen Mania Ministries is all about helping young people realize the power of the One who made them and the power of the one He made them to be. Here's what we do:

Teen Mania Global Expeditions. Thousands of young people are changing the world as they travel to thirty different countries for missions trips every year.

Acquire the Fire Youth Conventions. Teen Mania hosts weekly youth conventions across North America where teens learn about radical Christian living.

AcquireTheFire.com. Over nine million people visit our site each month to surf our devotions, chat rooms, and discussion boards.

Acquire the Fire Dome Events. Each year, Teen Mania hosts a dome event that challenges teens in their faith. In 1999 and 2000, over 70,000 teens and leaders attended the events at the Silverdome in Pontiac, Michigan.

Acquire the Fire TV Show. Ron Luce hosts a weekly program for teens that airs on several television outlets, such as the Trinity Broadcasting Network.

Teen Mania Honor Academy. Each year, high school graduates live on the Teen Mania campus in Garden Valley, Texas, for an exciting one-year program on faith, leadership, purpose, visions, integrity, and honor.

Extreme Camps. No other summer camp compares! Bands, speakers, intense spiritual growth and the most fun imaginable combined into one week.

GOD IS STRONG AND
CAN HELP YOU NOT TO
FALL. **HE CAN
BRING YOU
BEFORE HIS
GLORY WITHOUT
ANY WRONG IN
YOU AND CAN
GIVE YOU
GREAT JOY.**

—JUDE 24